By Richard Robinson

Robinson Children's Books

Dedicated to my computer and printer,
which proved the book by crashing a day before
the deadline.

More than that: dedicated to Thirzie, my wife,
who could have snapped, but didn't.

First published in the UK by Robinson Children's Books,
an imprint of Constable & Robinson Ltd, 2002

Constable & Robinson Ltd
3 The Lanchesters
162 Fulham Palace Road
London W6 9ER
www.constablerobinson.com

Illustrations & Text © Richard Robinson 2002

A copy of the British Library Cataloguing in Publication Data for
this title is available from the British Library.

ISBN 1 84119 547 2

Printed and bound in the EU

10 9 8 7 6 5

CONTENTS

WHY IS THE WORLD SO VERY WONKY?

We are ruled by a set of cast-iron laws which we can't dodge, however hard we try. Experts and teachers throw explanations at us, but they make no sense. Why should rubber ducks head straight for the tap? Why should the toast always land butter-side down? . . . why why why? This book is full of weird phenomena like these, but the reasons for the weirdness boil down to one: THE WORLD IS OUT TO GET YOU.

This fact was first noticed in a US Air Force base in California in 1949, and christened **Murphy's Law**. Since then it has been spotted in every aspect of life, in every corner of the globe. This book adds a few more laws to the swelling list of wonky laws, as well as selecting some of the most famous from the past.

In addition, there are tales from history, not about the famous figures we've all heard about, but their younger brothers, who get far too little attention, and whose lives were deeply wonky.

Good luck.

CHAPTER 1
SCHOOL

At school everything goes wrong. And it goes wrong in the wrongest way. And it goes wrong more when everyone is watching.

Cheer up. It's supposed to be like that. Let it all go wrong now, then when you leave school . . .

. . . well, it still goes wrong, but it goes wrong with so much more style.

CLASS PROJECTS

MURPHY'S LAW
If anything can go wrong
it will go wrong.

DEALING WITH MURPHY'S LAW
Trying to make things better only
makes things worse.

FELT PEN TIPS
Felt tip pens are all dry,
except for yellow ones.

LIBRARY RULES
The only book missing from the library is the
one you need for your project.

RULES OF GLUE

Glue . . .

1. sticks to skin but not to leather,

2. sticks to clothes but not to cloth,

3. sticks to books but not to paper.

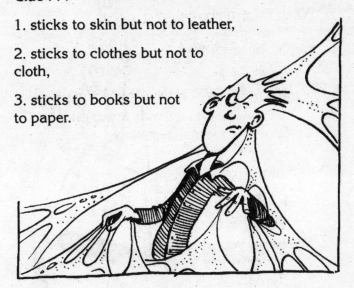

THE COMPUTER
The computer is placed
at the wrong end of the queue.

AND WHEN IT'S YOUR TURN, IT CRASHES

IRON LAW
OF NAILS

When fingernails are
needed
they've been chewed
away.

RULE OF
RULERS

Whatever you want
to measure is
1cm longer
than the ruler.

THE LAW
OF SMUG

Whatever happens,
there's always
someone who knew
that would happen.

THREE STAGES OF A PROJECT

"It's impossible."   "It won't work."   "It was my idea all along."

LENDING LAWS

1. When you lend something it disappears.

2. When you borrow something it disappears.

3. When you leave it alone it disappears.

THE LAST RESORT
If nothing else works,
try teacher's suggestion.

THE CLASSROOM

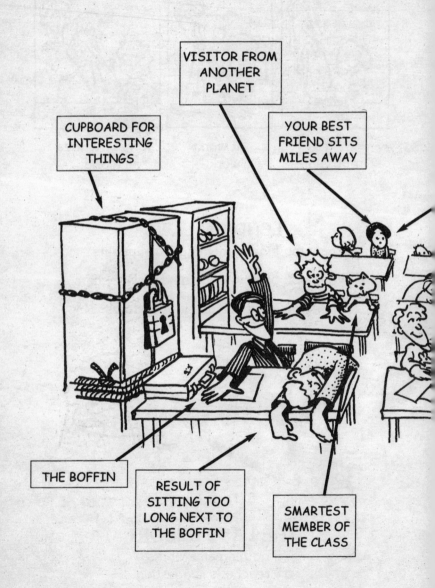

VISITOR FROM ANOTHER PLANET

CUPBOARD FOR INTERESTING THINGS

YOUR BEST FRIEND SITS MILES AWAY

THE BOFFIN

RESULT OF SITTING TOO LONG NEXT TO THE BOFFIN

SMARTEST MEMBER OF THE CLASS

LAWS OF SEATING

IF YOUR BEST FRIEND MOVES NEXT TO YOU, THEY BECOME YOUR WORST ENEMY IMMEDIATELY

THE BULLY SITS BEHIND YOU

YOUR WORST ENEMY SITS NEXT TO YOU

THE SUN IS IN YOUR EYES

YOU HAVE THE WORST TEACHER IN THE SCHOOL

BULLIES

Every class has a bully and a victim.

When you first arrive, check to see if you can spot the victim. If you can't, leave the school: you're the victim.

FIVE LAWS OF BULLIES

1. Never lend money to bullies.

2. Never.

3. Never.

4. Never.

5. Unless they ask.

TEACHERS

Teachers will give you all the time in the world
– keep it below three minutes.

Break time and lunchtime are the two times of
day reserved for teachers to relax.

Break time and lunchtime are the two times of
day reserved for teachers to rehearse plays,
meet parents, phone home, have staff
meetings, do playground duty.

After relaxing at lunch, teachers are at their
most dangerous.

THE CHANGING FACE OF TEACHING

Teachers have five faces.

1. **9.00 am** – the parents drop off their darlings.

2. **11.30 am**

3. **12.30 pm**

4. **2.30 pm**

5. **3.30 pm** – the parents pick up their darlings.

If you don't offer to help, teachers complain.

If you do offer to help, it's the wrong help.

Teachers on playground duty always spot the wrong crime.

AND **WHAT** ARE WE CHEWING?

LESSONS

Lessons would be over sooner if teachers taught what everybody already knows. The common sense curriculum which follows should replace the wonky one taught in schools.

ENGLISH

Of all the languages in the world, English is the one we all know already, so why is it the one taught in schools? Because it has been made deliberately difficult to learn.

When you want to say "uf", you write "ough" (as in "enough").

To say "oo", you write "ough" (through).

To say "or", you write "ough" (thought).

To say "off", you write "ough" (trough).

To say "ow", you write "ough" (bough).

To say "uh", you write "ough" (thorough).

When you want to say "ee" you can write either "ee", "ie", "ea", "y" or "i".

!!!!!!!!!!!!!!!!

There is an easier way . . .

(also an eesier way, iesier way, an ysier way and an isier way) . . .

The paragraph below has been written in the English of the future, with all the oddities removed.

- No double ll's, ee's, ss's, etc.
- No ough's
- Each letter has one sound only.

It's so much better than the old way, don't you think:

thy inglish langwij nyds to by thuruli overhorld. wuns orl the speling has byn simplifyd lyc this it wil imydyetly by sew much ysier to yus. meny kidz ar orlredy ryting lyc this. thei ar ahed ov the gaym.

Show this piece of writing to a teacher and watch them squirm. This is the way forward!

ENGLISH REPORT

Julian's spelling
is a~~troosh~~ ~~attrose~~
~~attroosh~~ ~~atroo~~shus
bad

GUIDE TO GREAT LITERATURE

1. When a book has no pictures it's good literature.

2. When it has no pictures and small print it's great literature.

3. When it's thick, with no pictures and small print it's a masterpiece.

4. When it's thick, small print, no pictures and in a foreign language, it's Shakespeare.

THIS'LL FIX 'EM, HAR HAR HAR HAR!

EDGAR ALAN'S POEM LAW

Poems that don't make sense
get better marks.

THE LAWS OF ESSAYS

1. The more work you put into an essay,
   the lower the mark.

2. Putting less work into an essay doesn't
   raise the mark.

THE LAW OF PUBLIC SPEAKING

When you have to read something aloud, the
words rearrange themselves on the page and
come out as rubbish.

In fact, whatever you say in public comes out
mangled (see Jessel's Law, p35).

GEOGRAPHY

The world is flat.

We know this because

1. It looks flat.

2. Otherwise all the water in the seas would pour away.

3. Whichever direction you go, it's never downhill (see Raleigh's Laws, p150).

THE WRONG SHAPE

WEATHER

The wind blows in your face.

Rain falls because you left your coat at home.

CLIMATE

All the other countries of the world have better climates than you do.

Until you visit them.

SCIENCE

THE SUN

The Sun goes round the Earth.

During the day the Sun travels at various speeds. It goes faster when you're having fun. Good days end sooner.

It doesn't go in a straight line. It can move to any position in the sky in order to shine in your eyes.

When you're indoors the Sun is out. As soon as you go out the Sun goes in.

It goes in faster if you were going to sunbathe.

If it's a blazing hot day and you've just walked three miles to the beach in nothing but your swimming gear with a picnic and a beach ball, ready for a day's fun at the seaside, the Sun is replaced by a thunder cloud and the sea freezes over.

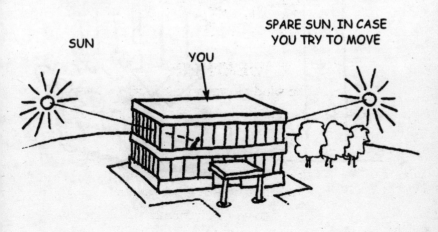

SUN

YOU

SPARE SUN, IN CASE
YOU TRY TO MOVE

GRAVITY

Gravity pulls in all directions. Flames are pulled upwards, so are short skirts during wedding photos. Gravity pulls sideways to get cups over the edge of the table on their way to the floor.

Gravity is stronger near cliff edges and at tops of stairs.

It is stronger in winter than summer. All the leaves are pulled off the trees, and the Sun can't climb so high in the sky.

Gravity is stronger first thing in the morning when you're trying to get up, and during games. It's particularly strong on Sunday after lunch when nearly all grown-ups are dragged down into the nearest sofa for hours.

SOUND

Loud sounds travel faster than quiet sounds.

Sounds travel along age bands. Sounds coming from parents and baby brothers are hardly audible.

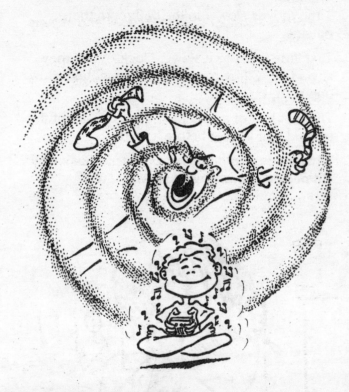

Some words are louder than others, some are softer. Words such as "telly", "pocket money", "sleep" are louder than words like "washing-up", "tidy", "your", "room", "come-back-here-this-minute".

TIME

Time is relative.

During boring lessons each second stretches to an hour. During interesting lessons an hour can squash up into five minutes.

Time moves slower in the bathroom than outside.

Taxi time is set to a slower clock. When they say a taxi will be round in three minutes, allow one hour.

The first half of a holiday takes forever, but the second half is over before it starts.

When you get old time goes faster. That's why old people seem to walk slowly.

GALILEO'S BROTHER

Galileo invented the clock, inspired by watching a church chandelier swinging like a pendulum during a three hour service. Not a lot of people know that Galileo's brother, Jock, watched the same chandelier as he did, but with a completely different effect.

OPTICS

As things go further away they appear smaller. If they're important they get bigger. Things shrivel up and disappear if you like them, and look bigger and more dangerous if you don't.

As younger brothers get nearer they become insignificant.

MAGNETISM

Magnets attract pieces of metal. They also attract sellotape, jam and the fingers of younger brothers. Older brothers' fingers are particularly hard to remove.

Clothes attract food. The more expensive the clothes, the stronger the magnetism.

Undersides of tables attract chewing gum.

Skin attracts dirt.

Shoes attract dog poo.

Adults are repelled by young people, and vice versa.

QUANTUM PHYSICS

Quantum scientists believe we live in one of a large number of parallel universes. Every time you make a choice between, say, five different actions, the other four choices are made in four different universes. They are good choices; the one you make in this universe is always wrong.

Some scientists believe that small objects can actually slip between universes, thus seeming to disappear for the length of time it takes to look for them, then reappear – exactly where they were – just after you buy a replacement (see also Schrödinger's Dog, p94).

QUANTUM ENTANGLEMENT

In the quantum world, instantaneous communication can happen between things even when far apart. This quantum entanglement can explain Glove Laws (see p166):

Why do gloves never match?

1. No two gloves in a pair occupy the same room.

2. As soon as one glove is found and is observed to be a right-hand glove, the other glove instantly becomes a right-hand glove.

CHAOS THEORY

Everything tends towards chaos.

UNCERTAINTY PRINCIPLE

One can never be certain
how much chaos.

EXPERIMENTAL LAWS

Experiments only work successfully
in the write-up.

HEALTH AND SAFETY

In science lessons, when nothing is going to
happen, you have to put on goggles, gloves
and crash helmets. In the playground, where
everything happens, you have none of these.

READY FOR
BREAK TIME

BIOLOGY

UNIVERSAL LAW OF ANIMALS

Animals larger than humans want to eat us.

Animals smaller than humans want to sting us.

USEFUL RULE FOR INSECTS

Some insects are brightly coloured to advertise that they taste unpleasant.

Insects that are not brightly coloured don't taste any better.

ENDANGERED SPECIES

Endangered species have fur, big eyes and cuddly names.

The Poisonous Marsh Liver Fluke is not so much endangered as doomed.

As soon as a species becomes endangered, fifty film crews rush in to trample its habitat flat.

GENERAL RULE OF SCIENCE

If it wriggles it's biology.

If it stinks it's chemistry.

If it doesn't work it's physics.

FAMOUS
LAST
WORDS

TRUST ME, I'M A
SCIENTIST.

HISTORY

THREE LAWS OF HISTORY

1. If it happened in the past, it's over by now. Don't trouble me.

2. If it's going to happen in the future, don't trouble me yet.

3. If it's happening in the present, you'd better get on with it and stop troubling me.

MATHS IN ONE

There are only three numbers:

one

two

lots

MATHS IN TWO

To some of us, all numbers are odd numbers.

ARTY FACT

The less time you take over a painting, the more likely it is to end up on the wall.

The same is true of the Royal Academy exhibition.

MUSIC

THE ONLY LAW

The only tunes that you can't get out of your head are the ones you shouldn't have let in.

BEETHOVEN'S BROTHER

Not a lot of people know that Ludwig von Beethoven was actually hopeless at music. His identical twin brother Geoffrey was the real genius. Ludwig used to bully Geoffrey. He locked him up in the cellar and forced him to write symphony after symphony, then Ludwig touted them around town as his own. Ludwig became famous, while Geoffrey starved.

One day Geoffrey escaped from the cellar. He rushed straight through town, heading for the concert hall. People stopped him in the street; "Hello, Ludwig, how are you?"

"I'm Geoff! I'm Geoff!", he answered.

"Sorry to hear about that," shouted the fans. "When did the trouble start?"

And so the story of Beethoven's deafness was born.

EXAMS

Exam questions are about:

1. the lesson you missed,

2. the topic your teacher forgot to cover,

3. the subject you didn't need to swot up because they NEVER ask that question.

LAWS OF THE EXAM ROOM

Everyone else knows the right answers.

EXAMS AND THE WEATHER

All through revision the weather is beautiful.
On the last minute of the last exam
the rain starts.

DON'T FORGET

If the answer was easy,
you read the question wrong.

GAMES

The more you need exercise,
the less you can do it.

FOOTBALL

1. When they pick teams, you are picked last.

2. The opposition are taller.

3. The player marking you has eight convictions for assault.

4. Nobody passes the ball to you.

   NOTE: When at last you do get the ball, it's vital not to pass it to anyone else.

5. On the coldest day you are in goal.

YOUR GOAL

THEIR GOAL

CRICKET MADE SIMPLE

*If you don't throw it,
they can't hit it.*

THE PLAY

The school play is never chosen because it's a good play but because it's got the right number of parts. The lead part never goes to the best actor, but to whoever is the right height. The songs never go to the ones who can sing, but to the kids who are tone deaf.

All acting obeys the law stated a century ago by Sir George Jessel.

JESSEL'S LAW
The human brain is remarkable; it starts working the moment you are born, and never stops until the first moment you have to stand up and speak in public.

AS THE CURTAIN RISES
1. the saliva leaves the mouth,
2. the brain leaves the head,
3. the safety pin leaves the back of your costume.

PUNCHLINE CRUNCHTIME
As you reach the punchline, all the mobiles in the audience go off.

GOING TO SCHOOL

Parents keep cool in the morning.

Until they get as far as the front door . . .

and they take it out on YOU.

DRIVING: KEY LAWS

1. Your parents don't realise their car keys are on the kitchen table until just after the front door closes.

2. The car keys are next to the front door keys.

3. If it's raining, their umbrella is next to the car keys.

4. If they want to phone for help, the phone is next to the umbrella.

TRAFFIC REGULATIONS

On the days that you are latest, the traffic is thickest.

WALKING TO SCHOOL

When you decide to walk, it decides to rain.

THE LAW OF BUSES

The bus to school is earlier every morning.

On the morning you get to the bus stop early enough, the bus is cancelled.

If you get to the stop on time and the bus is on time, don't take it: it's Sunday.

NATURAL HISTORY OF BUSES

Buses go round in threes.

DADDY BUS   MUMMY BUS   BABY BUS

CRIMINAL LAW

On the day the inspector gets on the bus, your ticket finds the hole between your pocket and the lining of your coat.

RUSH HOUR BUSES

The first bus is packed.

The second bus is empty.

You always take the first bus.

If you decide to take the second bus,
there is no second bus.

WHEN THE BUS DOESN'T
COME

If you decide to walk on to the next bus stop,
the bus will turn up when you are midway
between stops.

CHAPTER 2
YOURSELF

You are the most important thing in the universe. Other people might not know this yet. It's easy to feel that in your parents' list of important things you are number 347, just below "spare bag of cement".

On bad days, all the others in your family make you feel you are simply blocking the light.

It's not helped by <u>THINGS</u> WITH ATTITUDE.

When objects start to fight back, then you realise what a struggle you've got on your hands.

LITTLE NEMO'S BEDTIME LAW

Parents make you go to bed in the evening
when you are beginning to wake up properly,
then they wake you up in the morning
when you are tired.

BIG NEMO'S WAKE-TIME LAW

As soon as you turn on the light inside it
goes back to midnight outside.

This is another example of the flexibility of
time (see p22).

CLOTHES

There doesn't seem to be much that can go wrong with clothes, until you try getting them on in a hurry. Then you find all the nice ones are in the wash, apart from your very favourite, the one which your parents say you can't possibly wear because you're not going to be seen in public wearing THAT.

ST. ODDS LAWS OF SOCKS

1. You have an odd number of socks.

2. Of these, no two will make a pair.

SHOE SAVVY

If two shoes are left side by side overnight they will be found side by side in the morning . . .

. . . unless you need them.

The more urgent your need,
the further they fly apart.

WELLINGTON'S SHOE LAW

Shoelaces come undone.

Named after the Duke of Wellington, who beat Napoleon. Napoleon's famous saying was "an army marches on its stomach," which means "there's no point sending them to battle without a good meal inside them". Wellington realised that an army actually marches on its feet and invented the Wellington boot. With no laces to trip over, his soldiers won the battle of Waterloo before Napoleon's lot had finished washing up the breakfast things and done up their shoelaces.

PHILIP WELLINGTON

Not a lot of people know about Philip Wellington, who reckoned he could improve on his bro by doing away with not just the laces, but every part of the boot except the sole. He called his new creation the "Philip-phlop".

When the British army was equipped with philip-phlops it lost several battles in a row. Philip was sent away in disgrace and ended his days living in Clacton-on-Sea – where his philip-flops came in handy on the beach.

MOBIUS'S T-SHIRT PARADOX

The more careful you are to put a T-shirt on the right way round, the more likely you are not to manage it.

RAMSEY MACDONALD'S COLLAR CODE

Collars are either too loose or too tight.

JOHN LOGIE BAIRD'S BUTTON LAW

Left to themselves, buttons do up wrong. With your help, they do up wronger.

ADOLPH HITLER'S HAIR SECRET
One hair always sticks up.

The stray hair cost Adolph his job at
his dad's accountancy firm.
There's a lesson there for all of us.

CHAMBERLAIN'S PHONE LAW

You think of the most important thing to say
just after you put the phone down.

PARTY
PIECE PRINCIPLE

Nothing works when people watch.

DR SPOCK'S LAW OF
FAMILY LOVE

You give your toys to your younger sister
because it would be cruel not to.
You give your toys to your older brother
because he's bigger.

PERCY'S POSER

Why is belly button fluff always blue?

ILLNESS

COLDS LAW

1. Colds strike on the day before the school trip.

2. Recovery is complete on the evening before the maths test.

THE INVALID'S MOAN

On days when you miss school because of illness, parents insist you stay in bed as if you were sick or something.

DRACULA'S DENTISTRY ENIGMA

Toothache starts on Friday night.

THE PANIC PRINCIPLE

If you read a medical dictionary to check your symptoms you find that what you thought was acne is actually diphtheria,

or typhoid, or smallpox, or beri beri

or a broken ribcage, or a heart attack, or the end of the world.

The hospital tells you it's acne.

INVERSE LAW OF WAITING ROOMS

1. The more boring the magazines in the waiting room, the longer you have to wait for the doctor.

2. When it's your turn to see the doctor the symptoms disappear.

3. Just outside the door the symptoms return.

4. As you leave you spot a fascinating article in one of the boring magazines.

5. Two days later you go down with the flu you picked up in the waiting room.

CHAPTER 3
FAMILY

Kids aren't allowed to live without grown-ups. There is a reason: grown-ups would get lonely without young company. They need something to shout at, something to be cross about, something to put colour into their cheeks.

So remember, a parent is for life, not just for Christmas. Never let a day go by without showing them how much you care. Give them plenty of exercise.

Throw balls for them.

Play guessing games with them.

Help them practise their weightlifting.

Then they won't keep you awake half the night.

Parents say the opposite of what they mean:

THEY SAY	BUT THEY MEAN
"You're over-tired."	*"I'm over-tired."*
"Keep calm."	*"If you don't, I'll explode."*
"You won't feel a thing."	*"You will writhe in agony all the rest of your days."*
"Think nothing of it."	*"Repay me by Saturday."*
"The skin is the best bit."	*"I couldn't be bothered to peel them."*
"Computer games are bad for you."	*"It's my turn."*
"Thank you for washing up."	*"I'll clean up the floor, walls and furniture later."*
"Nearly there."	*"Three hours to go."*
"It's just around the corner."	*"I'm completely lost."*
". . . because I say so!"	*"I've forgotten what we were arguing about."*
"Rules are there to be obeyed."	*". . . except by me."*
"Come on in, the water's lovely."	*". . . if you've got skin like an elephant."*

THE PRINCIPLE
OF NAMING

They never call you by your name.

First parents give
you a name, then
they call you
something else all
your life. Jonathan
becomes Jo,
Elizabeth becomes
Betty, Philippa
becomes Pip. Why
don't they name
you what they
mean to call you
right from the
start?

I NAME THIS
CHILD, "OI YOU!"

HELP WITH HOMEWORK

Parents have three answers to difficult
homework questions: the sarcastic, the long
and the short.

e.g. You: "Dad, why did King Harold lose the
Battle of Hastings?"

> *Answer 1* (sarcastic): "I imagine he forgot
> where he left it, like you do."

> *Answer 2* (long): Well, it all goes back to
> the Viking settlement of Northern
> Europe in the ninth century . . ."

> *Answer 3* (short): "Because I say so."

PARENTS AND WEALTH

Parents are incredibly rich. They're made of money; you can hear it clanking in their pockets as they walk. Their wallets bulge with notes, each worth a dozen choccy bars.

Yet they give you NOTHING.

When you ask for a modest £3,000 they'll moan on and on about bills; mortgage, electricity, clothes, food, trivial things like that. Seconds later you'll find them spending freely on useless things like petrol or medicine, ignoring your pleas for a nuclear-powered bike.

Not content with merely depriving you, they torture you in several cruel ways:

1. The sweet shop

The average shop displays 2,056 things you are not allowed to have. Each is colourfully wrapped and dangled in front of your face. The parent's delight is to say "NO!" over and over for a full five minutes while they buy what they want, then fob you off with some 5p bauble.

2. Pocket money

There isn't anybody in the land who can say they get enough pocket money. Clearly the idea of such a paltry payment is to impress you with how rich the parent is, and how poor you look beside them.

3. Clothes

You are punished with clothes which are at least a week out of fashion.

4. Food

You are denied proper food. Anyone knows that the best things in life come in huge, classy packets that cost a fortune, and are covered in creamy, sugary, brightly covered, sticky, chocolatey, syrupy dollops of bite-sized bliss. Parents insist on giving you stuff that's "good for you"; things that dropped off a tree – "fruit" – or which they found in the ground – "vegetables". This is what humanoids were eating in caves 10,000 years ago. Have we not progressed since then?

5. Tips

Next time you eat out, notice that the waiter's tip is greater than your weekly pocket money. So your parents are willing to give more money to a total stranger they'll never meet again than to you.

Think about it.

CRIME AND PUNISHMENT

Of course you want to be good and do what's right, but you also want attention from your Mum and Dad. Trouble is that according to the WONKY LAW OF PARENTAL LOVE:

> Parents ignore you until
> you do something wrong.

So you can achieve one or the other, but not both. Whatever you do they'll tell you not to. If you say "but you did that yourself" they say

> "Don't do what I DO,
> do what I SAY!"

If you say "but I want to . . ." they say

> "I want never gets."

If you say "I wish I could . . ." they say

> "If wishes were horses,
> beggars would ride."

If you say "but I need it now!" they say

> "Patience is a virtue."

> "Everything comes
> to those who wait."

> . . . blah, blah, blah.

So you can't win. Your only hope is to lose creatively. Remember the great truths listed over the page.

DIRTY HARRY'S LAW OF NEED
It is easier to get forgiveness than permission.

NIXON'S LAW OF DISCOVERY
A simple lie is better than a complicated truth.

UNIVERSAL ALL-EMBRACING
LAW OF PARENTS
If parents shout at you,
it's because they're wrong.

If they don't shout at you,
it's because you're right.

MARK TWAIN'S INVERSION

As soon as you promise not to do something, you just have to do it.

ROMEO'S LAW OF DENIAL

The higher the shelf they put it on, the more you want it.

NO-WIN LAW OF VISITS

When you go visiting, you have to let them have their own way because you're a guest.

When others visit you, you have to let them have their own way because you're the host.

OLDER BROTHERS

- get better presents,
- watch what they want on TV,
- sit in the best chairs,
- have nicer clothes,
- don't have to eat up all their sprouts like you do,
- have their own way . . .

YOUNGER BROTHERS

- get better presents,
- watch what they want on TV,
- sit in the best chairs,
- have nicer clothes,
- don't have to eat up all their sprouts like you do,
- have their own way . . .

CHAPTER 4

HOME

Homes have more problems than you do. Look at it from the house's point of view. No sooner has it put on a new coat of paint or repaired its cracks than somebody ups and chips it or drills it. All it can do is sit there and take the attacks of the weather, the cats and the DIY enthusiast day in, day out.

It's not surprising if it takes it out on you.

KITCHEN

The kitchen is where good food goes to die. Your meals are cooked by people whose taste buds have been so shattered by years of abuse that they no longer understand what good food tastes like.

Proof of this is their liking for foul-tasting muck like coffee, beer, curry, chilli, chutney, pickle and broccoli.

Meals are always the wrong way round. The pudding should be first, with the main course fitting into any spaces left over. Everybody knows this. Even your parents knew this when they were your age. Yet as soon as they started cooking their own food they caved in to tradition and served it up with the pudding at the wrong end.

NEWTON'S NERD LAW

The toast always lands butter side down.

Perhaps the most researched law of all. Most
laws have the decency to operate secretly,
while your back is turned. This one is
shameless. Let a piece of toast slip off the
plate and just watch the insolence of the thing
as it rotates in mid-air, as calm as anything,
and plops on to the best carpet.

PERPETUAL MOTION

Scientists have designed a way to exploit Newton's Nerd Law and fulfil one of our great dreams – perpetual motion.

It is well known that cats always land on their feet. This can be linked to Newton's Law.

A piece of toast is strapped to the back of a cat, butter side up. The cat is dropped from 30cm above the floor. It will immediately spin round so that the butter side is down; then round again to land on its feet . . . and so on, neither side being able to hit the floor.

The cat will rotate just above the floor for ever.

ISAAC NEWTON'S BROTHER

Isaac spent many hours under an apple tree meditating on the laws of gravity.

Not a lot of people know that his brother, Eustace, also liked to meditate under a tree. Like Isaac he had some brilliant ideas.

Unfortunately he was under the wrong tree.

LUCIFER'S RULE

Toasters take two goes. The first leaves the
bread untouched, the second
scorches it black.

IVOR'S CUTLERY

The best cutlery is never used.

WOK LAW

You always cook too much rice.

THE LAW OF CAKE

When every one has politely taken the
smallest slice, the one that's left for you is the
smallest slice.

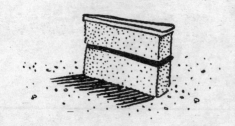

MARMITE MAGIC
The marmite jar is always empty.

In spite of this, there is always enough
for one more slice.

DESMOND'S DISCOVERY
Hot plates look exactly the same as
cold plates.

UH-OH

THE FRUIT ILLUSION
In any fruit the bruise is on the other side.
If you check both sides the bruise is
in the middle.

THE ALL OR NOTHING LAW
OF KETCHUP
Ketchup is all or nothing.

CONTAINER LAW
Only adults have difficulty
with child-proof containers.

MESSY EATER'S GUARANTEE
If the floor is dirty, food won't spill on it.

If it has just been cleaned, food cannot avoid
spilling on it.

GOOD FOOD GUIDE
The more it's good for you, the worse it tastes.

THE RULE OF SANDWICH
The hardness of the butter matches the
softness of the bread.

WASHING-UP

COMPLETION RULE OF WASHING-UP

There's always one teaspoon left in the washing-up bowl.

FUTILITY LAW OF WASHING-UP

When the washing-up is finally finished more dirty plates arrive.

FUTILITY LAW OF ARGUING ABOUT WASHING-UP

There's always an argument about washing-up, which you lose.

DISH-WASH HOG-WASH

Buying a dishwashing machine reduces the labour. Now the argument is about who presses the button.

BATHROOM

Is the house out to get you or not? The answer is right here in the bathroom. Packed out with smooth, slippery surfaces, sloshed with water. If you haven't slipped over yet, you will soon. Then you'll find out who's boss.

CLUSTER CUSTOM

1. Everyone wants to be in the bathroom at the same time.

2. When the bathroom is free, nobody wants to use it.

SOUTHSEA LAW OF BUBBLE BATHS

The bubbles end up behind you.

ARMAGEDDON RULE OF SPIDERS

Every day the spider in the bath gets bigger.

BORIS

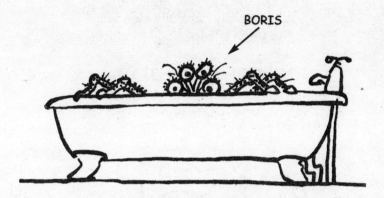

THE NARCISSUS LAW

Mirrors steam up as you want to use them.

THE TRADITION OF THE SOAP

There is a piece of soap by the sink which has been there untouched for three years because it's:

a) too small to use but

b) too big to throw away.

THE FLEXIBILITY OF TIME

How long a minute is depends on what side of the bathroom door you are on.

DUCK SUICIDE
The rubber duck swims straight under the tap.

FOOTBALL'S REVENGE
On the day the bathroom
is especially carefully cleaned,
the pitch is especially muddy.

ARCHIMEDES' LAW

When a body is immersed in water, the floor
gets a soaking.

ARCHIMEDES' BROTHER

Very little is known about Archimedes'
younger brother, Bertie. Archimedes became
famous by running down the street stark
naked. Bertie Mides, who couldn't run so fast,
was caught by Mum and made to clean up his
brother's mess in the bathroom.

THE RIDDLE OF THE
SHOWER TAP

Showers are either icy cold or boiling hot. To
get from one to the other, turn the tap
one millimetre.

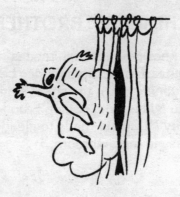

THE CLING FILM EFFECT

The shower curtain always wraps itself
around you.

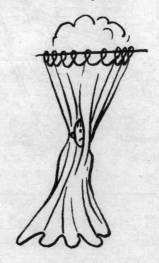

TOILET TISSUE TREACHERY

It is when you need to use the loo paper that you find it has been finished.

BEASTLINESS OF BOG ROLLS

The perforations don't match up.

WASHING MACHINE LAW

The whole load ends up inside the duvet cover.

THE GREAT TOOTHBRUSH TRUTH

There are twice as many toothbrushes in the bathroom as there are people in the house.

For keys, the figure is higher.

Much much higher.

CONFUCIUS' WISDOM ON TOOTHPASTE MANAGEMENT

Once the toothpaste has come out of the tube, it's hard to get it back.

PACKAGING PARADOX

Toothbrushes were never supposed to leave their wrapping.

FAMOUS LAST WORDS

THE FLOOR
SHOULD BE DRY
ENOUGH TO WALK
ON BY NOW.

GARDENS

Gardens are not havens of peace and tranquillity. Every plant is fighting to the death with its neighbours, trying to squeeze their roots and steal their sunshine. They are themselves being sucked dry by aphids, who are being munched by ladybirds, who are eaten by birds. The pretty little bird twitterings are alarm calls because the cat is about to eat them.

All in all it's safest to stay indoors. There may be noise and smell, but at least the fireplace doesn't spend its life plotting against the carpet, or the table throttling the chairs.

THE GREAT UNIVERSAL
LAW OF SHEDS

In every garden shed there is:

1. a bag of rock-hard cement,

2. a stick used for stirring paint in 1978,

3. 15 things that might come in useful one day, but haven't,

4. a paintbrush caked in paint, next to an unopened bottle of brush cleaner,

5. a piece of chicken wire that's too small to do anything with, but too big to avoid snarling your clothes on,

6. a flowerpot with a dead twig sticking out of it, waiting to be revived,

7. a rotten floorboard, just inside the door,

8. 300 packets of seeds (all open).

IDENTIFYING GARDEN PLANTS

Some plants grow easily in your garden. These are called "weeds".

Some plants grow with great difficulty. These are called "expensive".

Fruit and veg from the garden is covered in fungi, bugs and diseases. These are called "good for you".

PARENTS AND GARDENS

Grown-ups spend all day up to their elbows in soil, enjoying every minute, then scream at you for bringing a trace of it into the house.

LAWN LAW

When the grass is perfect the nice plants have gone.

THE PROBLEM WITH SOFT GRASS

The only time you can't play on the lawn is when you really want to.

ALEXANDER THE GREAT'S WHIM

The neighbour's garden is more interesting than yours.

TURF WAR LAW

Garden games end in tears.

FAMOUS
LAST
WORDS

I BET I CAN LEAN
OUT OF THE
WINDOW FURTHER
THAN YOU.

CHAPTER 5

PETS

Some bad luck waits for you to trip over it.
Some bad luck follows you around. That's
pets. But just because they make your life
wonky, that doesn't mean they aren't being
wonked just as much as you. Dogs are dying
to do a wee until you let them outside, then
the feeling goes and they want to come back
in. Cats are starving hungry until the tin is
opened, then their hunger vanishes. Have pity
on them.

But remain alert.

WHY PETS?

It seems strange that grown-ups spend years teaching their kids not to eat the furniture, stand on the sofa, make messes all over the beds, growl at visitors, etc. then buy themselves an animal which will do all those things. Why?

Were pets invented to give their owners something to talk to?

Is it so that they have something to go walkies with?

Do they have pets because they can't get on with humans?

Why do pet lovers have one pet too many?

We may never know.

MEDUSA'S FANCY

People who keep snakes like to make friends
with people who keep mice.

THESEUS' THESIS

People who keep mice should pick their
friends carefully.

HAMPSTEAD HAMPSTER LAW

Hamsters sleep all day.

As you start to go to bed,
they start to wake up.

LOOPY LUPUS LAW OF RABBITS

If you buy a pair of male rabbits, three weeks later one of the males has babies.

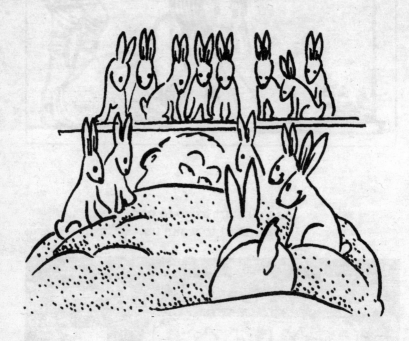

THE TRUTH ABOUT GUINEA PIGS

Guinea pigs are not as interesting as pigs or as useful as a guinea.

DELIA'S LAW

Cats know how much you spent on their food.

DOG LAWS

1. When the pet dog is most friendly, that is when it has managed to poo in the washing machine.

2. Puppies grow more than you expect.

SCHRÖDINGER'S LAW

No matter which side of the door the dog is on,
it's the wrong side.

SCHRÖDINGER'S DOG

Schrödinger was a famous nuclear physicist,
but not very good at looking after his pets.
When the neighbours complained about the
way he treated his cat (kept in a box with a
lump of uranium), he swapped it for two dogs.
He kept them in parallel universes – something
only a very advanced scientist could do (see
Quantum Physics, p25). But when he opened
the door he was never sure whether he was
letting one of them in or
the other one out.

Obeying Heisenberg's
Uncertainty Principle, he
regularly forgot whether he
had fed them or not, so
when he came down in the
morning it was a relief to
find they were still alive.

Or were they? . . .

DARROW'S MAXIM

The first half of our life is ruined by our parents, the second half by our children.

DARROW'S MUM'S NOTE

. . . and anything in between is ruined by our pets.

LAMARK'S THEORY OF EVOLUTION

Pet owners grow to look like their pets.

FAMOUS
LAST
WORDS

I OFTEN FORGET
TO FEED ZOLTAN,
BUT HE DOESN'T
SEEM TO MIND.

CHAPTER 6
TECHNOLOGY

You can't argue with technology, everybody knows that. What you may not know is that you can't break it either. You might think you can, but you can't. It breaks itself, and sometimes uses you to help.

Proof that it's out to get you: TVs break down as the deciding penalty is being taken; ovens pack up minutes before the party; the central heating pumps out heat all summer long, but at the first sign of a cold snap, there it goes; just before you press the 'save' button, the computer crashes. This is all predicted in Feydeau's Law.

FEYDEAU'S LAW
All gizmos break at exactly the worst time.

BUYING STUFF

Whatever you buy, the next shop
sells the same thing cheaper.

Not only that, next week it'll have
a new version which has twice
the power for half the price.

And that's what all
your friends will be buying.

And yours will be incompatible.

MANUAL LABOUR

Instruction manuals are either written in Japanese and translated into English by a monkey, or written in English and translated into Japanese, then back into English (removing the need for a monkey). This ensures they make more sense when read from the middle outwards.

INVERSE LAW OF MANUALS

Instructions have three pages telling you in detail how to open the packet, and four words on operating the software.

THE PATH OF PROGRESS

When you understand the manual completely the machine becomes obsolete.

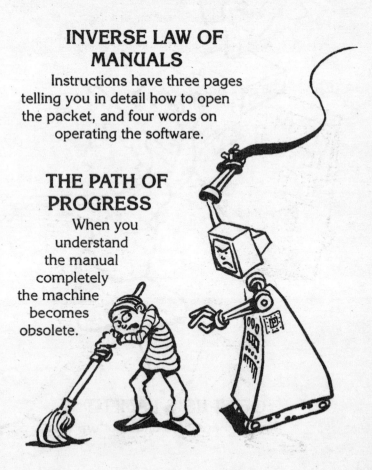

DEADLINE DICTUM
Never let a computer know
how much hurry you are in.

OEDIPUS'S LAMENT
In life there is no undo button.

DESIGN FAULTS

All technology sets out to deceive you. That TV screen is never 42cm wide, as the box says because what is printed on the box is the diagonal measurement, corner to corner.

Catches you every time!

THE DIAL SOLUTION
All the volume control on a stereo dial is covered between 5 and 6.

LIBERACE'S LAW
The more buttons and flashing lights, the less it can do.

SEEDY CDs
CDs never fly quite as well as you would expect.

VIDEO NUTCASE
The label on the video case tells you what is NOT inside.

KNOTTY PROBLEM
The number of knots in any collection of wires is found by multiplying the number of wires by the time in seconds that they have been touching.

RANSOM LAW

The one part that doesn't work is the thing that's not covered by the guarantee.

To make it work you need one extra cable.

The cable costs £250.

THE JUST-BEFORE-YOU-THROW-IT-OUT-OF-THE-WINDOW -IN-DISGUST-BECAUSE-IT-_WILL-NOT-WORK_ LAW

If all else fails, plug it in.

SELF-ASSEMBLY

THE DIY MANOEUVRE

When you have to assemble something from a kit, there's one bit left over at the end.

When you take it back to the shop, they look at you in a funny way and point out that half of it has been put together upside down.

When you put it together again the right way round, you find there's one piece missing.

You don't dare go back to that shop again.

BECKS' LAW
Battery holders lose their lids.

POSH'S PERPLEXITY
There is a drawer where interesting pieces of plastic are stored, in case a use is found for them. These are battery holder lids.

Nobody ever makes the connection.

YELTSIN'S LAW
A dead battery looks
exactly like a live battery.

TV CRIMES

The TV remote control is called "remote" for a reason: it's never where you left it. Frustrating isn't it. But spare a thought for the skill, energy, flair, patience and cunning shown by the plucky remote while it slips away from where it should be to where you wouldn't believe it possible to get. Enjoy the search. (All the normal rules for searches apply – see p123.)

BEETHOVEN'S LAW
The sound is always too quiet for you and too loud for Dad.

SCHEDULERS' REVENGE

All good programmes happen at the same time.

CUP FINAL CUSTOM

1. Goals are scored when you blink.

2. Five goals are scored while you are in the loo.

THE STEVEN KING EFFECT

Parents come in at the most violent moment of the video.

DEL BELL

Alexander Graham Bell's famous first line when he built his telephone was "Come here Watson, I want you." He had spilt some acid on his hand. From then on, you can imagine, Watson's life changed for ever. Bell was constantly on the blower to him for this or that. There seemed to be no escape.

Bell's younger brother, Del, had the answer to Watson's problem. His invention was the second great contribution to modern life . . .

BELL'S DISCOVERY

All the numbers you dial are engaged, unless they are wrong numbers.

GREMLIN'S LAW

Phone cables tangle up.

TRACEY'S LAW

Mobile phones are magnetically attracted to other people's pockets.

TOO FREE PHONE LAW

Cable free phones end up next to the TV remote (see TV CRIMES, p106).

THE STATING-THE-OBVIOUS LAW

Answer machines tell you
the number you have just dialled.

THE MARATHON LAW

When messages are to be taken,
the paper runs away from the phones,
the pens run away from the paper
and the ink runs away from the pens.

LIGHTS

THE ALL-OR-NOTHING LAW OF BULBS

When a bulb goes, if you leave it you have one dud light. If you replace it, all the other bulbs go and you have a houseful of dud lights.

ELECTRIC IRONY

The time you really really need light most is when hunting for a new light bulb.

LUIGI EDISON'S BRIGHT SPARK

One of the great inventions of the last millennium was Thomas Edison's electric light bulb. Not a lot of people know about his younger brother's contribution.

Luigi Edison knew that the task was not complete, and invented screw-fit bulbs. Up until that moment all bulbs had the same bayonet attachment. But from then on you could never be sure whether you were buying the right fitment. Thank you, Luigi!

LUIGI'S LAWS

1. The bulb you buy will be the wrong bulb.

2. If the bulb is right, the socket will be wrong.

GAMES

PELMAN'S TRUISM
Pelmanism: the same card
shows up all the time.

THE KING LEAR EFFECT
Playing Happy Families can destroy families.

DID I WIN,
THEN?

SPASKY'S CHESS LAW
Whoever you play is either much worse than
you or miles better than you.

MAYFAIR MURPHY LAW

If you have Mayfair with a hotel,
nobody lands on it.

If someone else has Mayfair with a hotel,
nobody but you lands on it.

VOILET ELIZABETH BOTT'S
LAW OF POKER

A temper tantrum beats a royal flush.

VAN GOGH'S UNIVERSAL
JIGSAW LAW

There's one piece missing.

CHAPTER 7

JOBS

There is always a list called "jobs to be done – urgent". Before life appeared on Earth there was a list of jobs to be done – urgent. Perhaps even before the Big Bang. It may be that the Big Bang itself happened because of something that hadn't been fixed yet.

Jobs appear in lists, towards the bottom, under "take terrapins for walk". The only way to get them to the top of the list is by turning the list upside down.

One of the lowest jobs is "TIDY UP – URGENT".

But this is impossible. The amount of untidiness in a house is fixed. The untidiness can be arranged in different ways, but it will never get smaller. For instance, in my house, tidying books away in one part of the house results in books in another part of the house falling off their shelf into a puddle of ketchup (see Quantum Entanglement, p25).

The wonky world doesn't allow tidy people. When people start being too tidy they get a pet.

DOUBTFIRE'S CONJECTURE

When Mum runs screaming round the house,
tidying up frantically, you know the
cleaner is coming.

WINDOW CLEANER'S DILEMMA

Spots on windows move from inside to the
outside and back again so you can
never catch them (see Quantum
Entanglement, p25).

KISSINGER'S INSIGHT

When something becomes clean, something
else has become dirty.

PANDORA'S LAW

Games never fit back in
their boxes.

THATCHER'S POT PLANT PRONOUNCEMENT

The uglier a household plant is,
the longer it survives.

HUBBLE'S CONSTANT

Matter expands to fill all flat surfaces.

DALEK'S RULE

Things with wheels
move to the top of the stairs.

ARMSTRONG'S "ONE-SMALL-STEP" ADDENDUM

Some things
without
wheels
move to
the bottom
of the stairs
minutes
later.

FLAT SURFACE MANAGEMENT

THE PAUL JONES PRINCIPLE

Everything is in the wrong place.

1. Before the kitchen things can be put on the kitchen table the toys have to be moved to the toy shelf,

2. so the CDs on the toy shelf must be moved to the CD rack,

3. so the books on the CD rack have to be moved to the bookshelf,

4. so the pot plants on the bookshelf must go back on the living room table,

5. so the kitchen things on the living room table go back to the kitchen table . . .

6. see 1.

Can the same be said of the Globe generally?

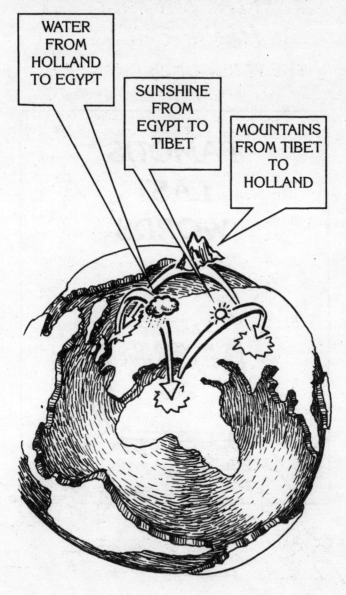

FAMOUS LAST WORDS

LOOK, I'VE MANAGED TO GET ALL MY TOYS ON TO THE TOP SHELF.

BIG EDDIE'S COIN LAW

The bigger the coin, the farther it rolls
under the freezer.

THE WILLIE WHITE LAW

There is a heavy, ugly, useless thing that sat in
the dark corner of a cabinet for twenty years.
The day after you throw it
away, you need it urgently.

PITFALLS RULES

Falling objects roll into a corner behind something.

If you listen out for where they fall, they fall silently.

If they are heavy they find your foot first.

If they are delicate they miss the carpet.

If they contain liquid, the liquid escapes.

If they are in a water-tight, shatter-proof container, the liquid spills out somehow.

On mopping up the liquid, you cut your hands on the fragments of shatter-proof container.

THE GROUNDHOG PRINCIPLE

When searching, you go back to the same place again and again.

On the twentieth visit, there it is!

(See Quantum Physics, p25)

DREYFUS'S LAW

The best way to find something is to accuse someone of nicking it. It will appear in the hand that's pointing accusingly.

RETROACTIVE SEARCH FORMULA

When you search,
you don't find what you are looking for.

You do find what you were looking for
last time you searched (but only if you've
bought a new one since then).

THESEUS'S SUPER-STRING THEORY

In any ball of string there are two ends. You
can only find one of them. But you find it
over and over again.

Shortly after you find the other end,
the third end appears.

COLUMBUS'S DISCOVERY

You always find things
in the last place you look.

I'M SURE I
LEFT IT HERE
SOMEWHERE.

MENDING LAWS

All things must break. When they break is a matter of timing – their timing, not yours; you have nothing to do with it.

Of course, everyone notices the sudden breakages. What few notice is the slow, creeping way things fall apart sneakily, when you aren't around (see Meldrew's Law of Lights, p136). This is called Incontinental Drift. It's very slow, but quite unstoppable.

For example, if an object has three components, they all move away from each other over many months to dark corners on opposite sides of the house, possibly near the TV remote (see p106).

There's a good reason why mending is a waste of time:

MEND A CITY

Before any item can be mended a new screwdriver/saw/micrometer screw-gauge will have to be bought. It will cost more than a replacement item.

Other reasons crowd out the next few pages.

BUSH'S OBSERVATION

It's easier to break something
than to mend it.

GENERAL RULE FOR FRIENDSHIPS, CIVILISATIONS, ETC.

See above.

CRAWFORD'S DICHOTOMY

There are two ways to approach a mending
job: your way and the correct way.

REPAIR ROLLER COASTER

Mending something when it is slightly broken
ensures it becomes completely broken.

When you throw it away you damage the bin.

Don't try to mend the bin.

TORQUEMADA'S TWIST

The last screw won't come undone.

THE SLOANE EFFECT
The more expensive the item,
the sooner it breaks.

FLINTSTONE FORMULA
Tough, heavy, unbreakable useful things break
sooner than flimsy, delicate, useless things.

THE TAY BRIDGE PARADIGM
Things break the day after
the guarantee runs out.

FRANKENSTEIN'S VERDICT
All tasks require one more
hand than is available.

THE WORK ETHIC

All jobs have four jobs connected on either side. For example if the door squeaks:

1. It must be removed from its hinges, which means

2. the screwdriver must be found, which means

3. the toolbox must be searched, which means

4. everything dropped into the toolbox over the past year must be returned to its proper shelf/hook/box.

(Time taken: three days)

When the door is ready to put back on its hinges:

5. longer screws are needed to fix it, then

6. the door frame has to be replaced, then

7. the wet rot behind the door frame must be cut away, then

8. the damp-proof course must be replaced and the central heating renewed.

(Time taken, four months)

BENTHAM'S REVENGE

The best way to repair something is to
get out all the tools,
then it will heal up without any help.

I JUST WANTED
TO KNOW YOU
CARED

AIRFIX LAW

When glue is used, the only things that don't
get stuck together are the two items you're
gluing (see Rules of Glue, p5).

FUTILITARIANISM

As soon as one thing is mended
three other things break.

DOUBLE-REFLECTIVE JOB LAW

If a job is hard it needs to be put off until there's plenty of clear time.

If a job is easy it can be left for a day or so.

OFF-PUTTING LAW

Any task worth doing is worth putting off till tomorrow.

CHAPTER 8
PARTIES

When grown-ups are preparing to have fun they are at their worst. Generally speaking, if you subtract the agony before and after a party from the pleasure during, you end up in the red.

When thirty of your friends are about to trash your house, why do the grown-ups rush around tidying it up so frantically?

VLAD THE IMPALER'S GUEST LAW

The one guest you'd like to leave first
stays until last.
The guests you like most can only stay
for half an hour.

DR WHO'S TIME LAW

One guest reads the invitation wrong and
arrives just after breakfast.

...AND BY THE WAY,
IT'S NOT FANCY DRESS

CHRISTMAS

Only three months of the year are not spent by shops advertising Christmas or Easter. These are spent advertising Mother's Day, Father's Day, Grandma's Day and Summer Holi Day, Why is there no day for you?

Try this: go up to Gran and say "Why is there a Mother's Day and a Father's Day, but no Children's Day?" She will reply – I promise you she will – "Every day is Children's Day."

SHERLOCK HOLMES' OBSERVATION

Father Christmas has the same handwriting as your parents.

MELDREW'S LAW OF LIGHTS

Between January and December, while carefully wrapped in tissue in a safe, clean, dry place, Christmas tree lights break.

CHRISTMAS TREE LAWS

It takes two hours to choose the Christmas tree. On the way home it grows too big or too small.

ST. SEBASTIAN'S LAW

Pine needles can't stay in the tree and they can't stay out of your socks.

The switch for the lights is in the middle of the tree.

When you turn the lights on, half the needles come off . . .

. . . in your hand.

TWELFTH NIGHT RULE

There's always one bit of decoration left on the wall after Christmas.

You find it after you've put the decoration box back at the far end of the loft.

PASSED PRESENTS

The present you like most breaks first.

The present you hate the most will last a thousand years.

Presents your parents approve of fall into the second group.

ONE FATHER CHRISTMAS
TOO FAR

Not a lot of people know about Father Christmas's brother. Wyatt Christmas set up a rival business at the South Pole, launching **newchristmas.com** in the middle of Australia's winter, on 21 June. His enterprise was not a success. Australians were very happy with Christmas where it was, in December, (mid-summer in Australia).

And anyway he kept giving people the wrong presents.

BUS LAW OF PARTIES
Parties are like buses: you wait
all year for one to come along,
then three happen on the same day.

CHARLES KENNEDY'S
PREDICAMENT
Everybody else's party is better than yours.

BABY'S VERDICT
The wrapping is more attractive
than the toy.

And lasts longer.

THE UNBREAKABLE TOY GUIDE
Unbreakable toys are useful for
breaking other toys.

BARBECUES

DANTE'S LAW
The worst cook in the world
finds work at a barbecue.

WATCHED POT LAW

(This law is equally true for barbecues
or bonfires.)

When it's not being watched, it goes out.

GAMOW'S BROTHER'S BIG BANGER THEORY

Not a lot of people know that while George Gamow was becoming famous with his Big Bang Theory for the origin of the universe his brother, Darren, was coming to another conclusion.

His Big Banger Theory states that everything started at a cosmic barbecue, when a gigantic sausage was put on the grill without being pricked first. The explosion that followed spread mess everywhere, one dollop of which became Earth as we know it.

Scientists have been slow to leap up and defend Darren's Big Banger Theory, but it has to be said in its favour that what it lacks in logic it makes up for in simplicity.

THE
BIG
BANGER

FAMOUS
LAST
WORDS

SPRINKLING A
LITTLE PETROL ON
THE CHARCOAL
HELPS TO GET THE
FIRE GOING.

CHAPTER 9

HOLIDAYS

If getting ready for a party is agony, multiply by a million to get an idea of holiday preparations. Parents become obsessed that if there's nobody in the house for a week it will most likely burn down or flood or collapse into disused mine workings. Bus-loads of friends and neighbours are forced to check on it every few minutes and feed the pets and slip in at night and switch lights on and off to deter burglars. And they mustn't find the place in a mess, must they, so the place is left cleaner than at any time while you were living there.

By the time you are ready to set off, the parents are exhausted and tetchy – in fact, you are all in need of a good holiday.

On holiday, they will twitch nervously. On the morning of the last day, they will at last relax and get into the spirit of the holiday. In the afternoon they start to pack again to go home.

Back at home there'll be the usual fortnight catching up on everything before life can settle back to normal again.

The holiday which took eight weeks to prepare and three weeks to recover from lasted five days.

TRAVEL

INVERSE LAWS OF SPEED

1. When you set out on holiday, so does everyone else.

   When you set off home again, so does everyone else.

   If you set off at 4.00 am to beat the rush, so does everyone else.

2. The faster you drive, the sooner you meet the tractor.

3. Short cuts are the longest routes.

NEARLY THERE

SHORT CUT

SLOWED RAGE

WHEN YOU ARE IN A HURRY on a motorway, the cones come out. Since they are the slowest moving things on the road (average speed 0 mph) they are mostly found in the fast lane. The traffic slows to a crawl.

Your lane crawls slowest (see QUEUES, p172).

As you enter the coned-off patch of the motorway where there is NO STOPPING, car sickness begins.

When accidents happen in the OPPOSITE carriageway, the traffic slows in YOUR carriageway as everybody cranes their necks to see what happened.

WHEN YOU ARE IN A HURRY on a narrow road, the big lorry pops up and crawls very, very slowly in front of you. When a chance to overtake comes up, it accelerates so you can't.

WHEN YOU ARE IN A HURRY in town, all the traffic lights are red and they stay red for longer.

You are, of course, ALWAYS IN A HURRY.

HENRY FORD'S YOUNGER BROTHER

Henry Ford's dream was that everybody should one day own a motor car. Not a lot of people know that his younger brother, Ron, had an even more splendid vision: that one day all the cars in the world would be joined together in a mighty river of steel. He experimented in 1913 by tying car bumpers together with rope, but his ideas were ahead of his day and drivers resisted. Nowadays, of course, we do it all the time. But while we celebrate John Ford, creator of the cheap car, nobody has a kind word for Ron Ford, inventor of the gridlock.

MAP LAWS

Large road atlases have only one page missing: the one you want.

City street guides have no pages missing, but the binding has come loose and the page order is random.

Town maps don't show the one-way systems, no-right-turns, pedestrianised areas, etc. So they are less use for finding your way about than a horoscope.

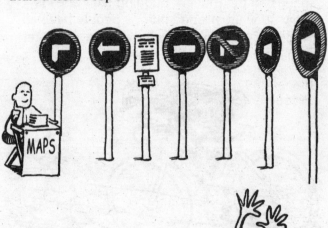

Open plan maps can't be refolded without using scissors.

CYCLING

To a cyclist, a pavement is a road with fewer cars. To a pedestrian, a cyclist is a car with fewer wheels.

The strangest thing is cycling fashion. Helmets are made streamlined to cut down on drag. This is useful if you cycle at the speed of sound. Proper cyclists have a skin-tight lycra cycling rig for the same reason. At normal speeds all the muscle-hugging stuff does is show up what strange bumps people have all over their legs. In general, the more go-faster stripes on a cyclist, the slower they go.

RALEIGH'S LAWS
In the presence of a bike,

1. all roads are uphill.

2. the wind is in your face.

3. the rain is up your nose.

WALTER RALEIGH'S YOUNGER BROTHER

Not a lot of people know that Edwin Raleigh brought back tobacco and potatoes from South America seven years before his brother Sir Walter.

But the tobacco tasted horrid and the potatoes wouldn't fit in his pipe, so he retired to Brighton where he built the world's first bicycle.

Unfortunately, in the sixteenth century, road-building technology was not ready for the Raleigh bike.

SUN DAZE

Parents always tell you to get out in the sun because it's healthy, then cover you with cream and hats because it's dangerous.

GRASS WARFARE

As soon as you lie down to sunbathe on the grass, all the insects in the world start to crawl over you.

If you look, they are gone.

If you keep your eyes shut, they stay, they grow extra claws, teeth and stings and invite their families to come play football in your armpits.

SUN-IN LAW

To guarantee hot weather, wear lots of pullovers.

THE COUNTRY

When you visit the country, the interesting wildlife has migrated to the town. Any that haven't left hide in the trees.

Country lovers will talk eagerly about conservation, searching among the roots of trees to find rats, mice, insects, algae. When they get home and find them living in the house, they'll do their best to kill them.

Of course, when you look at the countryside you never see anything happening at all. The really interesting time is after you've gone to bed, when all the mice, foxes, badgers, rabbits and deer wake up.

SISYPHUS'S HILL RULE

Hills have lots of tops. Every time you reach one, another appears higher up.

THE WASP

Scientists have studied wasps for any signs of purpose, and found none. What they have found is that wasps can smell jam from 15 miles away and, when you aren't watching, they sneak into your lemonade. So Mallory's Law of Wasps is proved.

MALLORY'S LAW

Wasps have no use except to sting you.

JEAN BRODIE'S LAW OF PICNICS
By the time you find the best spot for
a picnic lunch, it's supper time.

PICASSO'S PERCEPTION
When the picnic has been laid out,
the bull appears.

DUNKIN BUGS
When insects drown, they drown on
your side of the glass.

If you rotate the glass, the insect
stays on your side.

TANTALUS'S LAW
The best blackberries
are just out of reach.

The more you try to escape from the
brambles, the more you can't.

FAMOUS LAST WORDS

DON'T WORRY,
IT'S MORE
FRIGHTENED
THAN YOU ARE.

BEACHES

The best sandpaper is made by mixing towels with beach. Applied to the back and rubbed vigorously, this produces as good an effect as third-degree sunburn, and in a fraction of the time.

When you shake the towel to get the sand out, it goes straight into your eyes.

The sand that doesn't go in your eyes goes in the sandwiches. (Why did you think they were called sandwiches?)

In other countries they have a special word for large areas of barren sand. They call them deserts.

CANUTE'S TIDE LAWS

When you craft a delicate civilisation in sand, the tide comes right in over it.

When you build a mighty fortress against the sea, the tide goes out.

BADEN POWELL'S PRESCRIPTION
You are made to get into the sea when it's cold; you are made to get out again once it has become nice and warm.

SOUTHSEA BUBBLE LAW
Beachballs expire automatically after one day.

AMAZING NEWS!
Seaweed can be used to check for wet weather. If it goes soggy, expect rain.

YUP, IT LOOKS LIKE WE SHOULD EXPECT RAIN.

KRAY'S LAW OF URCHINS

Sea urchins know where you are.

THE SKIMMER'S DILEMMA

The best skimming stones are farthest from the water.

PHOAWRRR LAW

The stream on the beach that you like playing in comes straight from the hotel loos.

CAMPING

It is no coincidence that the word "tents" sounds like the word "tense". As you approach the campsite it starts to rain; if you decide to wait for the rain to stop it starts to get dark too.

Then you discover that all the tent poles are different lengths. Mathematicians have calculated that 10 tent poles can be arranged 3,628,800 ways, of which only one is correct. You will experiment with the other 3,628,799 ways. Eventually you discover which pole is the one you left at home.

Then you find that you only have half the tent pegs you need.

(When you pack up to go home you find 50 pegs left by the previous campers.)

On lighting your first campfire you discover the first law of camping:

STEPHENSON'S LAW
Campfire smoke always blows
in your face.

ERNEST STEPHENSON

Everybody knows about George Stephenson, inventor of the steam engine. Not a lot of people know about his younger brother.

Ernest Stephenson was committed to making everybody's Sunday complete by lighting a damp bonfire in his garden just before lunch. So successful was he that the neighbours from miles around made a collection to raise money to send him to America. Or Russia. Or anywhere. To transport his beloved bonfire he enlisted the help of his brother, George, who invented a device that puffed smoke all over the countryside. Thus began the great age of the train.

BERT WEEDON'S
JOLLY MUSIC LAWS

Wherever you camp, someone in a tent nearby
thinks they can play the guitar.

WEATHER

I'm not saying that weather is always awful.
Far from it. Sometimes it can be quite·
pleasant. But never when it's near you.

SAFE BET WEATHER FORECAST
Whatever the weather forecast says, the
opposite will happen.

... SO SUNSHINE EVERYWHERE TODAY ...

FIVE RULES OF RAIN

1. After the car has been cleaned, that's when it rains.

2. When the last item of the picnic has been laid out, that's when it rains.

3. When there's a full two miles between you and the nearest umbrella, that's when it rains.

4. When the wedding marquee has been taken down because the weather is so fine, that's when it rains.

5. When the whole festival has been crammed into the scout hut because the forecast was rain, that's when the Sun comes out.

THREE MORE RULES OF RAIN

1. If you wear protective gear, the rain falls horizontally.

2. If you protect yourself from horizontal rain, the rain falls upwards.

3. If you protect yourself from rain in any direction, the Sun comes out.

ONE MORE RULE OF RAIN

Rain is wetter when you go out into it.

DARWIN'S UMBRELLA LAW

In the end, umbrellas take on their natural shape, which is not the shape they sold to you.

WINTER WEAR

GLOVE LAWS
One glove is missing.

The only way to find it is to throw the other one away.

If the second glove is suddenly found, this will result in the instant thawing of all the snow.

BRUTE BOOT
Boots never quite match.

BRUTE SOCK LAW
When wearing boots, socks that aren't stapled on come off.

THE 99% LAW OF BOOTS
99% is fine. It's the 1% that leaks.

CARMEN MIRANDA'S HAT LAW
No parent looks good in a winter hat.

TOTAL WAR LAW
OF SNOWBALL FIGHTS
Just when you have enough ammunition,
the game is banned.

SPLINT'S LAW

The best part of a toboggan run is
just before
you spot
the tree.

CHAPTER 10

TRIPS

As you get ready for a trip into town,
remember to say farewell to thè money in your
pocket; once you leave home it'll pour out of
your pocket so fast that you won't have time
to wave it goodbye. And it will head straight
for the priciest shops and the worst deals,
where it will slip into a till, leaving you holding
a pink fluffy monstrosity which you thought
was IT five minutes previously. Even if you buy
nothing you'll get no change back.

LOOKING GLASS MONEY

The more you've got the more you spend. If you leave home with £5 in your pocket, you'll need £7. Leave home with £7 and you'll want £10. To be safe, leave home with £15. Then you'll need £20. No matter what you take, it won't be enough.

Strangely, shops don't advertise how much money you are about to spend. They tell you how much you will save. It can come as a shock that after a day doing nothing but save money in the shopping mall you are bankrupt.

HUGE SAVINGS!

...BUT THINK HOW MUCH WE SAVED!

THE LEWIS CARROLL
LAW OF SHOPPING

The bigger the bargain, the more
money leaves your pocket.

LEWIS CARROLL'S MUM'S
DEFLATION LAW

As soon as you buy something,
its value drops by half.

PENNY-PINCHING LAW

All items in a shop are short of a sensible
price by 1p.

FOR SALE
ONLY
£999,999.99

THE VERSAILLES PRINCIPLE

The more expensive a gadget,
the less you use it.

QUEUES

One of the most famous of Murphy's laws, proved time and again in every supermarket in the world:

MURPHY'S QUEUE LAW
The other queues move faster.

SECONDARY LAWS OF QUEUES

1. Swapping queues reverses the trend.

2. As you get to it, the shortest queue becomes the longest.

3. As you get to the till you remember the thing you forgot.

4. The thing you forgot is at the other end of the shop.

5. By the time you get back your queue has become gigantic.

STYLE & FASHION

It has never made sense that the most expensive clothes have the manufacturer's name all over them. You are no more than a walking billboard! You've just paid out pots of money to advertise their product! THEY should be paying YOU!

THE SINDY SYNDROME
The most fashionable clothes are the most uncomfortable.

THE WINDY SYNDROME
When you are looking your best, a cold wind springs up and you have to wear an anorak.

LAW OF FASHION BUYING

1. If you like it they don't have it in your size.

2. If you like it and they have it in your size, it doesn't fit anyway.

3. If you like it and they have it in your size and it fits, it's too expensive.

4. If you like it and they have it in your size, it fits, and it's not too expensive, it falls apart before you get home.

VOLTAIRE'S MOTTO

When kids show their independence by
dressing different, they all look the same.

LEIBNITZ'S RESPONSE

When you buy something that nobody else is
wearing, suddenly everyone is wearing it.

LAW OF SUPPLY AND DEMAND

Your size has just sold out.

The very last one went to the person in front of
you in the queue.

AQUINAS'S LAW OF PINS

All new shirts have a hidden pin. If you buy a
shirt that hasn't, it will grow one by next week.

SWIMMING

Straight away swimming pools show they're out to get you. If they didn't want you to crack your skull they would have carpet on the floors, not tiles.

When you get into the water, you discover that it's deeper than it looks. Scientists call this an optical illusion, but we all know what's going on here: it's out to get you.

Whenever you're standing in the pool, look down – you'll see the floor slopes up away from you. Try it: you'll see I'm right. Wherever you stand it's uphill in all directions (see Raleigh's Laws, p150).

LUCIFER'S LAW
Either the hot pool is too hot
or the cold pool
is too cold.
Or both.

DOUCHE'S LAW
The shower stops after three seconds.

GOOSE-BUMP CONVENTION
No matter how hot the shower,
you are always cold afterwards.

DR FOSTER'S ADVICE
The puddle sits below where your sock is
going to drop.

TAP DANCE ROUTINE
Taps in public places are push-button.

Sinks in public places have no plugs.

Hand-washing in public places is impossible.

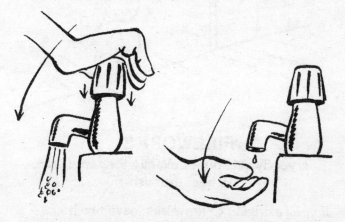

DRIER CONSEQUENCES
Automatic driers automatically
put a damp patch on your wrists.

LIBRARY LAW
The library is closed on the day you visit.

DOUBLE DOOR DUPLICITY
If the right door is unlocked, you pick the left.
If the left is unlocked, you pick the right.
If it's a pull, you push it.
If it's a push, you pull.
If there's no door at all, you walk into
the plate glass wall.

FIREWORKS
Everybody sets out at exactly the same time,
to beat the rush.

If you're driving to fireworks leave two hours –
one hour to sit in a traffic jam facing away
from home, and one more hour to do the same
facing towards home.

THEME PARK RIDE RULE

If the ride is good the queue is too long.
If the queue is short enough the ride's
not worth going on.

AWNING WARNING

Shop awnings protect you from the rain until
you try to leave them.

THEATRE LAW
People with seats in the middle arrive last

CINEMA LAW
The biggest hairstyle sits in front of you.

They arrive at the last minute
so you can't change seats.

*FAMOUS
LAST
WORDS*

I DON'T HAVE
TO LOOK; ON
A ZEBRA
CROSSING
IT'S MY RIGHT
OF WAY.

CURRY CODE

You wait years for an Indian Restaurant, then three open up at once.

(See also Natural History of Buses, p38 and Bus Law of Parties, p140)

BEELZEBUB'S LAW OF PAVING

The safest looking paving stone is the one that's going to squirt water up your leg.

THE APOLLO 11 CERTAINTY

When farthest from home you remember you left the grill on.

CHAPTER 11

CONCLUSION

The Red Queen summed it up in *Alice in Wonderland*: "It takes all the running you can do just to keep in the same place." Well, that's just the half of it. The wonky world is not just upside down, it's inside out as well. The faster you go, the slower you get, the farther up you climb, the lower down you find yourself. However hard you try, it all ends up topsy-turvy. In fact, put simply:

THE WORLD IS INDEED OUT TO GET YOU!

FAMOUS
LAST
WORDS

THERE'S PLENTY
OF ROOM IN
THE BACK.

Smarties Books are:
Fun, colourful, interactive,
imaginative, creative, wacky and
there's lots in them.

Other books available

Wizard Jokes ☐

A new and fizzing collection of spell-binding gags.
ISBN: 1-84119-383-6
Price: £2.99

Smarties Pirates ☐

All aboard for great adventures with big bad pirates!
ISBN: 1-84119-548-0
Price: £3.99

Smarties How To Be Really Smart ☐

. . . without really trying. Your supercool instant
guide to just about everything!
ISBN: 1-84119-461-1
Price: £3.99

Smarties Guide to the Galaxy ☐

Heaps of amazing facts, jokes and puzzles, on this
whirlwind tour of the galaxy and beyond.
ISBN: 1-84119-625-8
Price: £3.99

TBS Direct
Colchester Road, Frating Green, Colchester,
Essex CO7 7DW
Tel: +44 (0) 1206 255777
Fax: +44 (0) 1206 255914 Email; sales@tbs-ltd.co.uk

UK/BFPO customers please allow £1.00 for p&p for the
first book, plus 30p for each additional book up to a
maximum charge of £3.00.
Please send me the titles ticked.
Overseas customers (inc. Ireland), please allow £2.00
for the first book, plus £1.00 for the second, plus 50p
for each additional book.

NAME (Block letters) ....

ADDRESS..

....

....

POSTCODE ....

I enclose a cheque/PO (payable to TBS Direct) for ....

I wish to pay by Switch/Credit card ....

Number ....

Card Expiry Date...

Switch Issue Number ....